DISCOVERING AMERICAN DIALECTS

ROGER W. SHUY
Michigan State University

SPONSORED BY NCTE COMMISSION ON THE ENGLISH LANGUAGE

NATIONAL COUNCIL OF TEACHERS OF ENGLISH
1111 Kenyon Road   Urbana, Illinois 61801

NATIONAL COUNCIL OF TEACHERS OF ENGLISH

Foreword

The Committee on Publications of NCTE is pleased to offer to the profession this second practical classroom work on the varieties of English spoken by Americans. The publication is sponsored by the Commission on the English Language. An earlier Council publication, *Dialects U.S.A.*, by Jean Malmstrom and Annabel Ashley, suggested many classroom practices for introducing students to regional dialects. This volume by Professor Shuy extends the treatment of the earlier book and makes use of more recent research in linguistic geography, relying especially on more detailed geographical knowledge, recent studies of urban dialects, and a more precise appraisal of social dialects. As of September 1967, Dr. Shuy is Director of Urban Language Study and Materials Information Center at the Center for Applied Linguistics in Washington, D.C. With the growing attention to the study of the English language in our schools, the publication should provide teachers with a valuable resource.

JAMES R. SQUIRE

Chairman

Contents

Introduction

This book assumes that accurate statements about American English may be made only with an accurate *description* of American English. The study of the dialects of present-day American English is involved in such a description. Statements about the regional and social distributions of pronunciations, words, and grammatical forms are becoming available to the teachers and students of our country. *Discovering American Dialects* will show how these statements are made and will acquaint the high school student with some of the results.

The student of dialects does not make guesses about the regional and social varieties of the language. He gathers his data systematically and draws his conclusions from the evidence. The reader of this book is given many opportunities to engage in linguistic *fieldwork*, the kind of work that advanced students have done. He too will be able to gather data and draw conclusions based on evidence, not guesswork or prejudice.

It is hoped that this activity will result in a healthy attitude toward the English language. An understanding of our fellow man has frequently been hampered by prejudices about his language. Students of American English learn that there are different standards of acceptability in different parts of the country—that in many ways proper Boston English is not the same as proper Denver speech. It is further hoped that the reader will come to appreciate the richness of American dialect variations and that, as he is shown some differences between educated and uneducated speech, he will be better able to adapt his own speech to a given situation without scorning those who cannot do so successfully.

I. Dialects: What They Are

Many Americans are unaware that they and their friends speak a variety of English which can be called a dialect. Many even deny it and say something like this: "No, we don't speak a dialect around here. They speak more harshly and strangely out East and down South, but we just don't have anything like that in *our* speech."

Most Southerners know that people from other parts of the country are either pleased or annoyed by their Southern pronunciations and expressions. Many Easterners are aware of the reactions of people from west of the Alleghenies to typical Eastern speech patterns. On the other hand, many Midwesterners, for some reason, seem oblivious to the fact that Americans from other areas find something strange about the vocabulary, pronunciation, and grammar characteristic of the Midwest.

People tend to describe the differences between their speech and that of others in certain conventional terms. *Harshness* and *nasalized drawl* are often used to describe the speech of any area other than that of the speaker. Another popular term, *guttural,* is also used with little precision. Strangely enough, many people will insist that they hear a *guttural* quality in the speech of another person *even though they cannot define the term.*

Linguists who specialize in the study of dialects describe American speech systematically and with precision. They avoid terms like *harsh* and *dull,* for such words are closer to condemnation than description, and terms like *soft* and *musical,* for they are too general to be useful. Like many common English terms, these words have been used so widely that it is difficult to say exactly what they *do* mean.

How, then, can linguists go about describing dialect differences systematically and precisely? Perhaps we should begin with what we already know. In an age in which people often move from one area of the country to another, it is rather common for us to have neighbors or classmates whose dialect may be somewhat "different." Furthermore, the summer (or winter) vacation has enabled many of us to enter different dialect areas. Television and radio have brought speakers from many social and geographical dialect areas into our homes. We may begin, then, by recognizing that there *are* dialect differences.

1

Besides the facts, however, we also begin with attitudes. Since language is a form of social behavior, we react to a person's speech patterns as we would react to any of his actions. If his dialect differs from our own, we may consider him quaint, naive, stupid, suave, cultivated, conceited, alien, or any number of other things. Most frequently, however, our attitude toward the outsider tends to be negative, since, after all, he is not one of *our* group. Recently a graduate school professor at a large Midwestern university asked his students to describe various unidentified persons whose voices were recorded on tape. The class described one voice as rustic and uncultivated. The voice was that of their professor!

It is clear, then, that most people recognize dialect differences of some sort and have certain feelings or attitudes toward them. A classic example of this recognition and reaction occurred during a survey of Illinois speech conducted in 1962. Many people from the middle of the state and most from the southern part pronounced *greasy* something like *greezy*. On the other hand, people in the northern counties of the state pronounced the word *greecey*. The northern Illinois informants felt that the southern pronunciation was crude and ugly; it made them think of a very messy, dirty, sticky, smelly frying pan. To the southern and midland speakers, however, the northern pronunciation connoted a messy, dirty, sticky, smelly skillet.

Which of the two pronunciations and reactions are right? The answer is easy: The southern Illinois pronunciation and reaction are appropriate in southern Illinois, and the northern Illinois pronunciation and reaction are proper in northern Illinois. Educated *and* uneducated speakers say *greezy* in southern Illinois. Educated *and* uneducated speakers say *greecey* in northern Illinois. Although we must not be surprised that people tend to believe their own way is the "right way," it should be clear that there are two acceptable pronunciations of this word in Illinois, reflecting different dialects.

The word "dialect" is associated with speech communities, groups of people who are in constant internal communication. Such a group speaks its own dialect; that is, the members of the group have certain language habits in common. For example, a family is a speech community; the members of the family talk together constantly, and certain words have certain special meanings within the family group. The people who belong to your class in school form a speech community, sharing certain special ways of talking together—the latest slang, for instance. The people who work together in a single office are a speech community. Larger speech communities may be the members of a single occupation or profession. Carpenters share certain typical carpentry terms; lawyers use special legal terms.

An even larger speech community is made up of people who live in a particular geographic region. Such regional speech communities are the special concern of this book. The study of these communities is called "dialect geography" or "linguistic geography" or, simply, "dialectology." The scholar who studies varieties of a language is called a "dialect geographer," or a "linguistic geographer," or a "dialectologist."

Dialectology is concerned with the regional and social aspects of language. The intermingling of these regional and social aspects is clearly illustrated in American English. We are all aware of the fact that relatively uneducated people tend to use certain pronunciations, grammar, and vocabulary which easily identify them as uneducated. We know, furthermore, that people from certain areas speak in such a way that we can make a good general guess as to where they are from. The speech of any such person, then, is a mixture of social and geographical features. The educated person will undoubtedly share some of the geographical features found in the speech of his uneducated townsman, but he will probably *not* share the speech features which label the other man uneducated (at least not in his more formal utterances). Here we discover two different aspects of dialectology—*regional dialects* and *social dialects*.

We might say that there are at least three degrees of understanding of what dialects are. First, some people think that a dialect is something spoken by a white-bearded old man in an out-of-the-way area.

Once we became aware of the fact that we *all* speak a dialect of some sort, we recognize dialects in a geographical sense, the second degree of understanding.

The third degree of understanding comes when we realize that social layers exist *within* regional dialect areas. That is, well-educated, partly-educated, and uneducated people may all live within the boundaries of a well-defined dialect area. In one sense, they all speak dialect X. It is also true, however, that they speak different varieties of this dialect. Certain aspects of the dialect are shared by all social levels; others are used by only one or two of the groups.

A case in point is the past tense of the verb *climb*. Well-educated people in all dialect areas favor *climbed* as the past tense form. Some uneducated speakers in certain Northern dialect areas may say *clim*.

In some parts of the Midland and Southern dialect areas, many uneducated speakers say *clum;* in Virginia, many uneducated speakers say *clome.* With this verb, then, we find dialect variants only among uneducated speakers. The variants, *clim, clum,* and *clome,* have geographical *and* social patterns. Both must be taken into account.

A dialect, then, is a variety of a language. It differs from other varieties in certain features of pronunciation, vocabulary, and grammar ("grammar" will be used to mean both word construction *and* syntax). It may reveal something about the social or regional background of its speakers, and it will be generally understood by speakers of other dialects of the same language.

II. Dialects: How They Differ

We have said that speakers of one dialect may be set off from speakers of a different dialect by the use of certain pronunciations, words, and grammatical forms. The frequent first reaction of a person who hears an unfamiliar dialect is that the strange sounds and words are a chaotic mess. This is similar to the feeling an American has when he sees British motorists driving "on the wrong side of the street," or to the bewildered feeling we have upon hearing a foreign language for the first time. Surely, we feel, there is no system in that sort of behavior!

Mankind apparently views all unfamiliar human behavior as suspicious and unsystematic. If you have ever watched a bird build a nest on a window sill or in a bush within the range of any passing alley cat, you have probably not questioned the intelligence of the bird. Most people accept even apparently erratic animal behavior and assume that, no matter how foolish the act may seem, it probably makes sense to the animal. But as soon as a human being is seen to behave "differently," he is frequently considered foolish or uncooperative. Language, in this case a dialect, is also a form of behavior. That people speak different dialects in no way stems from their intelligence or judgment. They speak the dialect which enables them to get along with the other members of their social and geographical group.

DIFFERENCES IN PRONUNCIATION

Differences in pronunciation are of two types: totally patterned and partially patterned. A totally patterned difference is one in which the sound behaves consistently in a particular situation. For example, in some parts of the country, particularly in eastern New England, the pronunciation of "r" is lost before consonants and in word-final position. Thus a Midwesterner's "park the car" becomes the New Englander's "pahk the cah." From the New Englander's point of view, it might be equally valid to say that Midwesterners insert r's before consonants (park) and following a vowel at the ends of words (car). That the words in question have r's in their spellings is really not important here, for spellings remain fixed long after pronunciations change, and letters may have different sound values in different dialects. But whether we say the New Englander

5

drops an r or the Midwesterner *inserts* one, the fact remains that the difference is totally patterned in most speech styles. Recent dialect research has shown that a person may shift his pattern slightly, depending upon his relationship to his audience and on whether he is reading aloud or speaking impromptu. Professor William Labov of Columbia University has observed, for example, that New York working-class people tend to say *dis* for *this* and *dese* for *these* when they are talking about a bad accident or about a personal brush with death. They say *dis* and *dese* less frequently when talking with teachers and even less frequently when reading aloud.

The second kind of variation in pronunciation, a partially patterned difference, may occur in a few words or even in only one. The partially patterned sound is not consistent throughout the dialect. It was mentioned above that the eastern New Englander "drops" an r before consonants and in word-final position in a totally patterned way. Now let us cite the Midwesterner who inserts an r in certain words but in no particular phonetic pattern. In most of Ohio, Indiana, and Illinois (except for a few northern counties), *wash* is pronounced *"worsh"* by a large number of speakers, particularly by those with no more than a high school education. If this were totally patterned, these speakers would also say "bo*r*sh" instead of *bosh* and "jo*r*sh" instead of *josh* (many of them *do* say "go*r*sh" instead of *gosh*).

Other examples of partially patterned differences (still sticking with r problems) include "lozengers" for *lozenges*, "framiliar" for *familiar*, "quint*r*uplets" for quintuplets, and "su*r*press" for suppress. This phenomenon, sometimes referred to as the "intrusive r," is most noticeable in someone else's dialect. Midwesterners are amused at the Bostonian's pronunciation of "Cube*r*" and "Asia*r*" for Cuba and Asia before words beginning with vowels, failing to hear their own intrusive r's in *worsh* and *lozengers*. Likewise, the Bostonian tends to hear the Midwesterner's intrusive r's but not his own.[1]

Our standard alphabet cannot record the many sounds in American English pronunciation. The dialectologist uses a highly detailed phonetic alphabet to record the most minute audible features of speech. The student can easily learn and use a simpler set of symbols

---

[1] The "intrusive r" is not limited here to word structure but may be found in a string of sounds in a sentence. The Bostonian's "intrusive r" is either the last sound of a word which comes before a word beginning with a vowel or the last sound of an utterance.

to record the variations he meets in his dialect studies. Below is a chart which should enable you to record pronunciations yourself.

Consonants

Most of the consonant letters of our standard alphabet may be used to approximate the sounds we hear. Some new symbols are necessary, however, and these will be set off to the right and identified by a convenient label. Note that a key word is given to illustrate each sound.

Symbol	Key Word
p	pin
b	bin
t	tin
d	din
k	kin
g	get
m	man
n	nan
ŋ (eng)	sing
l	lip
r	rip
h	hat
w	win
y	yellow
θ (theta)	thin
ð (eth)	then
f	fish
v	very
s	sit
z	zip
č (c wedge)	church
ǰ (j wedge)	jail
š (s wedge)	share
ž (z wedge)	azure

Vowels

The vowels of English are much more difficult to represent because our alphabet provides only five symbols for a great many sounds. To understand why we need more phonetic symbols than letters in our alphabet, a cutaway drawing of the mouth may be helpful (Example 1).

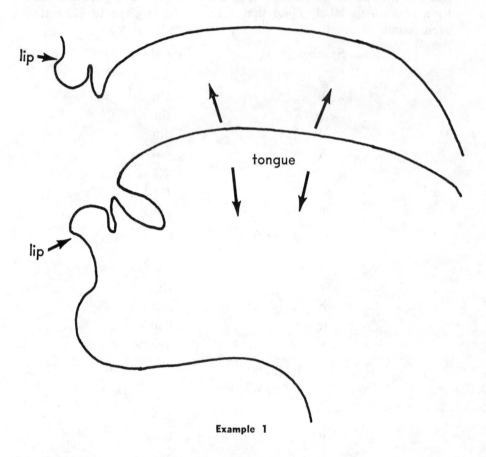

Example 1

Differences in vowels are made by raising, lowering, fronting, and backing the tongue and by spreading or rounding the lips. Thus a high front vowel is made with the tongue raised and fronted (see the upper dotted line in Example 2). A low back vowel is made with the tongue drawn back and flattened as low as possible (see the lower dotted line in Example 2).

A systematic way to identify vowels, then, is to describe the relative position of the tongue while they are being made. The following chart will show these positions and illustrate conventional

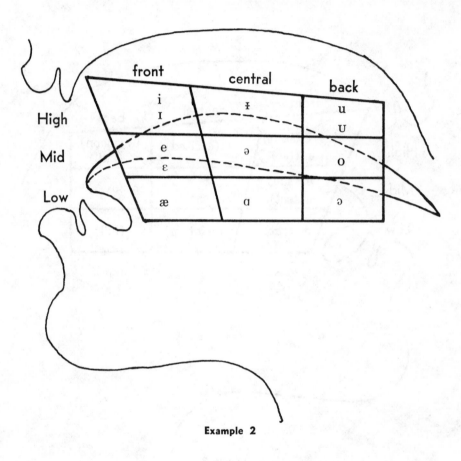

Example 2

symbols used for them. In order to better realize the sounds presented in Example 3, we can insert key words which may illustrate these sounds. Several words of warning must precede such an undertaking, however. The key words may not perfectly illustrate the sounds in your own dialect. The low central vowel, [ɑ], is used in *father* in most dialects, but some speakers will say it with an [ɔ]. Likewise, few speakers of American English can keep from gliding from [e] to [ɪ] in words like *say* or *bait,* or from gliding from [o] to [ʊ] in *over* or *boat.* But, for purposes of convenience, our key words will not reflect the natural tendency to glide these words.

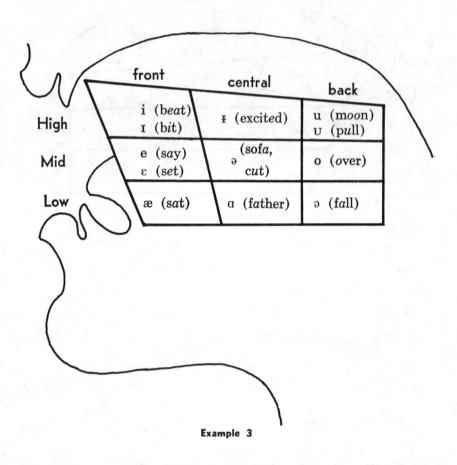

	front	central	back
High	i (b*ea*t) ɪ (b*i*t)	ɨ (exc*i*ted)	u (m*oo*n) ʊ (p*u*ll)
Mid	e (s*ay*) ε (s*e*t)	ə (s*o*fa, c*u*t)	o (*o*ver)
Low	æ (s*a*t)	ɑ (f*a*ther)	ɔ (f*a*ll)

Example 3

Certain vowel sounds of English are made up of combinations of the preceding sounds (Example 3). These are often called diphthongs or glides. Note the following examples:

Symbol	Key Word	Glide
aI	ride	from low central to lower high front
aU	cow	from low central to lower high back
ɔI	boy	from low back to lower high front

As your ability to hear and record speech sounds improves, you will be able to distinguish other glides such as the Midland [æʊ] in cow [kæʊ] as opposed to the Northern pronunciation [kaʊ].

Of course the professional linguist uses many more symbols because his ear is trained to hear minute distinctions; for your purposes, however, this basic list should be sufficient.

Pronunciation Fieldwork

As you practice writing the sounds you hear with the symbols listed on preceding pages, you can start to determine certain things about other speakers. Begin by writing short words, dictated by your teacher or your classmates. *Do not be influenced by the spelling of the word.* Listen only for its sound and write it using the phonetic symbols. People do not hear sounds in exactly the same ways, so it should not surprise you if the students in a given class produce several different acceptable transcriptions. The following words will provide good practice for you:

coat	ringing
cats	wilt
boom	late
beans	hike
catches	then
thick	should
sox	money
dogs	rumor
how	joy
boil	judges

Remember that a good ear for sounds is not developed right away. You may wish to practice with other transcription exercises, or you may simply write phonetically the words used by teachers, classmates, television performers, or members of your family. If classmates or friends from a different part of the country are willing to serve as informants, have them pronounce the following words:

Word	*Northern*	*Midland*	*Southern*
1. creek	ɪ and i	ɪ (north Midland) i (south Midland)	i
2. penny	ɛ	ɛ	ɪ—(Southwest)
3. Mary	ɛ e (parts of eastern New England)	ɛ	e
4. married	æ (east of Appalachians) ɛ (elsewhere)	ɛ	ɛ
5. cow	ɑU	æU	æU or ɑU
6. sister	ɪ	ɨ (eastern)	ɨ (eastern)
7. foreign	ɔ	ɑ	ɑ
8. orange	ɑ (east of Alleghenies) ɔ	ɑ and ɔ	ɑ and ɔ
9. tomato	o	ə	o or ə
10. coop	u	u (NM), U (SM)	U
11. roof	U	u and/or U	u
12. bulge	ə	ə or U	ə or U
13. farm	ɑ	ɑ or ɔ	ɑ or ɔ
14. wire	ɑɪ	ɑɪ or ɑ	ɑ

Word	Northern	Midland	Southern
15. won't	ə o (urban)	o ɔ	o ɔ
16. fog	ɑ (New England) ɑ and ɔ (Midwest)	ɔ	ɔ
17. hog	ɑ (New England) ɑ and ɔ (Midwest)	ɔ	ɔ
18. on	ɑ	ɔ	ɔ
19. long	ɔ	ɔ	ɑ (eastern Virginia) ɔ (elsewhere)
20. careless	ɨ	ə	ɨ
21. stomach	ə	ɪ	ə

The vowels of these words are pronounced differently in the various parts of our country. The major variants are listed beside the words along with their general distributions (for a map of the Northern, Midland, and Southern dialect areas, see page 47).

Consonants sometimes will give clues to the dialect a person speaks. The following generalizations may be helpful:

Word	Northern	Midland	Southern
1. humor	hɪumər	yumər	hɪumər or yumər
2. wash	wɑš or wɔš	wɔrš or wɔɪš	wɔš or wɔɪš or wɑš
3. with	wɪð and wɪθ (N.Y., Chicago, Detroit=wɪt working class)	wɪθ	wɪθ
4. greasy	grisɪ	grizɪ	grizɪ
5. barn	bɑrn (Eastern North=bɑn)	bɑrn	bɑrn (East Coast=ban)
6. these	ðiz (N.Y., Chicago, Detroit=diz working class)	ðiz	ðiz
7. which	hwɪč	wɪč	wɪč
8. miss	mɪs	mɪs	mɪz
9. Mrs.	mɪsɨz	mɪsɨz	mɪzɨz or mɪz

With the mobility of the American population today, we are bound to discover exceptions to generalizations like these. Also, as we shall see later, settlement history has caused some curious mixtures of speech patterns in our country. On the whole, however, the generalizations may be useful in helping you to recognize the dialect of your informant.

One bit of advice as you get your informants to say these words— *try for a natural situation.* One way professional fieldworkers have done this is to ask, for example, for what the person calls a small stream of water that runs through a farm. *Creek* is a likely response. You can easily invent similar questions for other words. It might be interesting, furthermore, to compare a person's response in conversation with his pronunciation when he reads the word in a sentence or in a list of such words. You may discover that your classmates have different pronunciations for different occasions.

There are two recordings you can use for practice, or just for listening to differences. One, *Americans Speaking*, is published by the National Council of Teachers of English, with six long selections spoken by educated adults. The other is *Our Changing Language*, published by McGraw-Hill (Webster Division), containing twelve short selections spoken by junior high school and high school students. Other recordings are in prospect.

DIFFERENCES IN VOCABULARY

Words are interesting to almost everyone. Through his vocabulary a person may reveal facts about his age, his sex, his education, his occupation, and his geographical and cultural origins. Our first reaction may be to imagine that all speakers of English use the same words. Nothing could be further from the truth; our language contains a vast number of synonyms to show different shades of meaning or reveal as much of our inner feelings as we want to. Some of these vocabulary choices are made deliberately. We use other words, however, without really knowing that our vocabulary is influenced by our audience.

Age

Certain words tell how old we are. For example, many people refer to an electric refrigerator as an *ice box* despite the fact that in most parts of our country ice boxes have not been in common use for many years. Older natives of some Northern dialect areas still may call a frying pan a *spider*, a term which remained in the vocab-

ulary of the older generation long after the removal of the four legs
which gave the descriptive title. Frying pans no longer look like
four-legged spiders, but the name remains fixed in the vocabulary
of certain people.

Sex

Our vocabulary may also identify whether we are male or female.
Most high school boys, for example, are not likely to use *lovely*,
peachy, *darling*, and many words ending in *-ie*. Adult males are not
apt to know or use very many words concerned with fabrics, color
shadings, sewing, or women's styles. Women of all ages are not
likely to use the specialized vocabulary of sports, automobile repair,
or plumbing.

Education

A person also reveals his educational background through his
choice of words. It is no secret that learning the specialized vocabulary of psychology, electronics, or fishing is necessary before one
becomes fully accepted as an "insider," and before he can fully
participate in these areas. Much of what a student learns about a
course in school is shown in his handling of the vocabulary of the
subject. It is also true, however, that a person's choice of words is
not nearly as revealing of education as his grammar and pronunciations are.

Occupation

The specialized vocabulary of occupational groups also appears
in everyday language. Truck drivers, secretaries, tirebuilders, sailors,
farmers, and members of many other occupations use such words.
Linguists who interview people for *The Linguistic Atlas of the United
States and Canada* have found that the calls to certain animals, for
example, illustrate what might be called farm vocabulary, particularly
for the older generation of farmers (city dwellers obviously have no
particular way of calling sheep or cows from pasture). Even within
farming areas, furthermore, vocabulary will reveal specialization.
Recent Illinois language studies showed that a male sheep was
known as a *buck* only to farmers who had at some time raised sheep.

Origins

It is common knowledge that certain words indicate where we
are from. Northerners use *pail* for a kind of metal container which

Midlanders refer to as a *bucket*. *Pits* are inside cherries and peaches of Northerners; *seeds* are found by some Midlanders. It is amusing to some people, furthermore, that as a general rule horses are said to *whinny* or *whinner* in Northern dialect areas, whereas they *nicker* in some of the Midland parts of our country.

Customs are also revealed in our vocabulary. The *county seat* is relatively unknown in rural New England, where local government is handled at the town meeting.

The special names for various ethnic or national groups, whether joking or derogatory, are an indication of the settlement patterns of an area. If a person has the terms *Dago*, *Kraut*, or *Polack* in his active vocabulary, it is quite likely that he lives among or near Italians, Germans, or Polish people. Sometimes the nickname of a specific immigrant group becomes generalized to include most or all newcomers. Such a case was recently noted in Summit County, Ohio, where some natives refer to almost all nationality groups as *Hunkies*, regardless of whether or not they come from Hungary. That this practice has been with us for many years is shown in a comment by Theodore Roosevelt that anything foreign was referred to as *Dutch*. One nineteenth century politician even referred to Italian paintings as "Dutch daubs from Italy." [1]

Vocabulary Fieldwork

To show some of the ways a speaker's vocabulary may reveal his age, sex, occupation, or regional and cultural origins, let us do a dialect vocabulary project as it might be done by a linguist (called a fieldworker in this case) who interviews people (called informants) for *The Linguistic Atlas*.

The Atlas fieldworker gathers his information in face-to-face interviews. He may supplement his interview data, however, with questionnaires such as the one which follows. Sometimes these questionnaires are mailed; sometimes the fieldworker distributes them personally. Whatever method of distribution is used, one thing is certain: The questionnaires have been extremely helpful, reliable, and accurate indications of vocabulary in use.

---

[1] H. L. Mencken, *The American Language*, abridged and revised by Raven I. McDavid, Jr. (New York: Knopf, 1963), p. 371.

A CHECKLIST OF REGIONAL EXPRESSIONS

DIRECTIONS

1. Please put a circle around the word or words in each group which you ordinarily use (don't circle words you have heard—just those you actually use).

2. IF the word you ordinarily use is not listed in the group, please write it in the space by the item.

3. IF you never use any word in the group, because you never need to refer to the thing described, do not mark the word.

EXAMPLE

CENTER OF A PEACH: pit, seed, (stone,) kernel, heart

HOUSEHOLD

1. TO PUT A SINGLE ROOM OF THE HOUSE IN ORDER: clean up, do up, redd up, ridd up, straighten up, tidy up, put to rights, slick up

2. PAPER CONTAINER FOR GROCERIES, ETC.: bag, poke, sack, toot

3. DEVICE FOUND ON OUTSIDE OF THE HOUSE OR IN YARD OR GARDEN: faucet, spicket, spigot, hydrant, tap

4. WINDOW COVERING ON ROLLERS: blinds, curtains, roller shades, shades, window blinds, window shades

5. LARGE OPEN METAL CONTAINER FOR SCRUB WATER: pail, bucket

6. OF PEAS: to hull, to pod, to shell, to shuck

7. WEB HANGING FROM CEILING OF A ROOM: cobweb, dust web, spider's web, web

8. METAL UTENSIL FOR FRYING: creeper, fryer, frying pan, fry pan, skillet, spider

9. OVER A SINK: faucet, hydrant, spicket, spigot, tap

10. OVERLAPPING HORIZONTAL BOARDS ON OUTSIDE OF HOUSE: clapboards, siding, weatherboards, weatherboarding

11. LARGE PORCH WITH ROOF: gallery, piazza, porch, portico, stoop, veranda

12. SMALL PORCH, OFTEN WITH NO ROOF: deck, platform, porch, portico, step, steps, stoop, veranda, piazza

13. DEVICES AT EDGES OF ROOF TO CARRY OFF RAIN: eaves, eaves spouts, eavestroughs, gutters, rain troughs, spouting, spouts, water gutter

14. RUBBER OR PLASTIC UTENSIL FOR SCRAPING DOUGH OR ICING FROM A MIXING BOWL: scraper, spatula, kid-cheater, bowl scraper

15. VEHICLE FOR SMALL BABY: baby buggy, baby cab, baby carriage, baby coach

16. TO_____THE BABY (IN SUCH A VEHICLE): ride, roll, wheel, push, walk, stroll

17. FURRY STUFF WHICH COLLECTS UNDER BEDS AND ON CLOSET FLOORS: dust, bunnies, dust kittens, lint balls, pussies

FAMILY

18. FAMILY WORD FOR FATHER: dad, daddy, father, pa, papa, pappy, paw, pop
19. FAMILY WORD FOR MOTHER: ma, mama, mammy, maw, mom, mommer, mommy, mother
20. IMMEDIATE FAMILY: my family, my folks, my parents, my people, my relatives, my relations, my kin, my kinfolks
21. OTHERS RELATED BY BLOOD: my family, my folks, my kind, my kinfolks, my people, my relation, my relatives, my relations, my kin
22. OF A CHILD: favors (HIS MOTHER), features, looks like, resembles, takes after, is the spitting image of
23. OF CHILDREN: brought up, fetched up, raised, reared
24. THE BABY *MOVES ON ALL FOURS* ACROSS THE FLOOR: crawls, creeps

AUTOMOTIVE

25. PLACE IN FRONT OF DRIVER WHERE INSTRUMENTS ARE: dash, dashboard, instrument panel, panel, crash panel
26. AUTOMOBILE DEVICE FOR MAKING THE CAR GO FASTER: accelerator, gas, gas pedal, pedal, throttle
27. PLACE WHERE FLASHLIGHT AND MAPS MAY BE KEPT: glove compartment, compartment, shelf, cabinet
28. AUTOMOBILE WITH TWO DOORS: tudor, coupe, two-door
29. THE CAR NEEDS_____: a grease job, greased, lubrication, a lube job, to be greased, to be lubed, greasing, servicing, to be serviced
30. LARGE TRUCK WITH TRAILER ATTACHED: truck, truck and trailer, semi, rig, trailer–truck

URBAN

31. NEW LIMITED ACCESS ROAD: turnpike, toll road, freeway, parkway, pay road, tollway, thruway, expressway
32. SERVICE AND EATING AREAS ON THE ABOVE: service stop, service area, oasis, rest area
33. GRASS STRIP IN THE CENTER OF A DIVIDED ROAD: median, center strip, separator, divider, barrier, grass strip, boulevard
34. PLACE WHERE FIRE ENGINES ARE KEPT: fire hall, fire house, fire station

35. PLACE WHERE SCHEDULED AIRLINES OPERATE: airport, port, terminal, air terminal, (by proper name), air field, field

36. PLACE WHERE TRAIN STOPS: station, railway station, depot, train stop, train station, railroad station

37. PLACE WHERE FIREMEN ATTACH HOSE: fire hydrant, fire plug, plug, hydrant, water tap

38. GRASS STRIP BETWEEN SIDEWALK AND STREET: berm, boulevard, boulevard strip, parking, parking strip, parkway, sidewalk plot, tree lawn, neutral ground, devil strip, tree bank, city strip

39. CALL TO HAIL A TAXI: taxi!, cab!, cabbie!, hack!, hey!, (wave arm), (whistle)

40. POLICEMAN: cop, policeman, copper, fuzz, dick, officer, bull

41. THE ROAD IS _____: slick, slippery

42. PLACE WHERE PACKAGED GROCERIES CAN BE PURCHASED: grocery store, general store, super market, store, delicatessen, grocery, market, food market, food store, super mart

43. A PIECE OF PAVEMENT BETWEEN TWO HOUSES ON A CITY BLOCK: gangway, walk, path, sidewalk

44. PLACE WHERE YOU WATCH TECHNICOLOR FEATURES IN A CAR: drive-in, drive-in movie, outdoor movie, outdoor theater, open-air movie, open-air theater, passion pit

NATURE

45. ANIMAL WITH STRONG ODOR: polecat, skunk, woodspussy, woodpussy

46. SMALL, SQUIRREL-LIKE ANIMAL THAT RUNS ALONG THE GROUND: chipmunk, grinnie, ground squirrel

47. WORM USED FOR BAIT IN FISHING: angledog, angleworm, bait worm, eace worm, earthworm, eelworm, fish bait, fishing worm, fishworm, mudworm, rainworm, redworm

48. LARGER WORM: dew worm, night crawler, night walker, (Georgia) wiggler, town worm

49. DOG OF NO SPECIAL KIND OR BREED: common dog, cur, cur dog, fice, feist, mongrel, no-count, scrub, heinz, sooner, mixed dog, mutt

50. INSECT THAT GLOWS AT NIGHT: fire bug, firefly, glow worm, june bug, lightning bug, candle bug

51. LARGE WINGED INSECT SEEN AROUND WATER: darning needle, devil's darning needle, dragon fly, ear-sewer, mosquito hawk, sewing needle, snake doctor, snake feeder, sewing bug

52. FRESHWATER SHELLFISH WITH CLAWS; SWIMS BACKWARD: crab, craw, crawdad(die), crawfish, crayfish

53. CENTER OF A CHERRY: pit, seed, stone, kernel, heart

54. CENTER OF A PEACH: pit, seed, stone, kernel, heart

55. HARD INNER COVER OF A WALNUT: hull, husk, shell, shuck

56. GREEN OUTER COVER OF A WALNUT: hull, husk, shell, shuck

57. BUNCH OF TREES GROWING IN OPEN COUNTRY (PARTICULARLY ON A HILL): motte, clump, grove, bluff

58. WEB FOUND OUTDOORS: cobweb, dew web, spider nest, spider's nest, spider web, web

59. TREE THAT PRODUCES SUGAR AND SYRUP: hard maple, rock maple, sugar maple, sugar tree, maple tree, candy tree, sweet maple

FOODS

60. MELON WITH YELLOW OR ORANGE INSIDES: muskmelon, melon, mushmelon, lope, cantaloup, mussmellon

61. A SPREADABLE LUNCHEON MEAT MADE OF LIVER: liver sausage, braunschweiger, liverwurst

62. A CARBONATED DRINK: pop, soda, soda pop, tonic, soft drink

63. A GLASS CONTAINING ICE CREAM AND ROOT BEER: a float, a root beer float, a black cow, a Boston cooler

64. DISH OF COOKED FRUIT EATEN AT THE END OF A MEAL: fruit, sauce, dessert, compote

65. PEACH WHOSE MEAT STICKS TO SEED: cling, cling peach, clingstone, clingstone peach, hard peach, plum-peach, press peach

66. FOOD EATEN BETWEEN REGULAR MEALS: a bite, lunch, a piece, piece meal, a snack, a mug-up, munch, nash, nosh

67. CORN SERVED ON COB: corn-on-the-cob, garden corn, green corn, mutton corn, roasting ears, sugar corn, sweet corn

68. BEANS EATEN IN PODS: green beans, sallet beans, snap beans, snaps, string beans, beans

69. EDIBLE TOPS OF TURNIPS, BEETS, ETC: greens, salad, sallet
70. A WHITE LUMPY CHEESE: clabber cheese, cottage cheese, curd cheese, curd(s), dutch cheese, home-made cheese, pot cheese, smear-case, cream cheese
71. ROUND, FLAT CONFECTION WITH HOLE IN CENTER, MADE WITH BAKING POWDER: crull, cruller, doughnut, fat-cake, fried-cake, cake doughnut, raised doughnut
72. BREAD MADE OF CORN MEAL: corn bread, corn dodger(s), corn pone, hoe cake(s), johnnycake, pone bread
73. COOKED MEAT JUICES POURED OVER MEAT, POTATOES, OR BREAD: gravy, sop, sauce, drippings
74. GROUND BEEF IN A BUN: hamburg, hamburger, burger
75. LARGE SANDWICH DESIGNED TO BE A MEAL IN ITSELF: hero, submarine, hoagy, grinder, poor-boy

GAMES

76. CHILDREN'S CRY AT HALLOWEEN TIME: trick or treat!, tricks or treats!, beggar's night!, help the poor!, Halloween!, give or receive!
77. FAST MOVING AMUSEMENT PARK RIDE (ON TRACKS): coaster, roller coaster, rolly-coaster, shoot-the-chutes, the ride of doom
78. CALL TO PLAYERS TO RETURN BECAUSE A NEW PLAYER WANTS TO JOIN: allie-allie-in-free, allie-allie-oxen free, allie-allie-ocean free, bee-bee bumble bee, everybody in free, newcomer-newcomer!
79. CALL TO PASSER-BY TO RETURN A BALL TO THE PLAYGROUND: little help!, ball!, hey!, yo!, ball up!
80. TO COAST ON SLED LYING DOWN FLAT: belly-booster, belly-bump, belly-bumper, belly-bunker, belly-bunt, belly-bust, belly buster, belly-down, belly-flop, belly-flopper, belly-grinder, belly-gut, belly-gutter, belly-kachug, belly-kachuck, belly-whack, belly-whop, belly-whopper, belly-slam, belly-smacker
81. TO HIT THE WATER WHEN DIVING: belly-flop, belly-flopper, belly-bust, belly-buster
82. TO STOP A GAME YOU CALL: time!, time out!, times!, pax!, fins!

SCHOOL

83. TO BE ABSENT FROM SCHOOL: bag school, bolt, cook jack, lay out, lie out, play hookey, play truant, run out of school, skip class, skip school, slip off from school, ditch, flick, flake school, blow school

84. WHERE SWINGS AND PLAY AREAS ARE: school yard, playground, school ground, yard, grounds

85. HOLDS SMALL OBJECTS TOGETHER: rubber band, rubber binder, elastic binder, gum band, elastic band

86. DRINKING FOUNTAIN: cooler, water cooler, bubbler, fountain, drinking fountain

87. THE AMOUNT OF BOOKS YOU CAN CARRY IN BOTH ARMS: armful, armload, load, turn

CLOTHING

88. SHORT KNEE-LENGTH OUTER GARMENT WORN BY MEN: shorts, bermuda shorts, bermudas, walking shorts, knee (length) pants, pants, knee-knockers

89. SHORT KNEE-LENGTH OUTER GARMENT WORN BY WOMEN: shorts, bermudas, walking shorts, pants

90. OUTER GARMENT OF A HEAVY MATERIAL WORN BY MALES AS THEY WORK: levis, overalls, dungarees, jeans, blue jeans, pants

91. GARMENT WORN BY WOMEN AT THE SEASHORE: swim suit, swimming suit, bathing suit

92. GARMENT WORN BY MEN AT THE SEASHORE: swim suit, swimming suit, bathing suit, swimming trunks, trunks, bathing trunks, swimming shorts

MISCELLANEOUS

93. A TIME OF DAY: quarter before eleven, quarter of eleven, quarter till eleven, quarter to eleven, 10:45

94. SOMEONE FROM THE COUNTRY: backwoodsman, clodhopper, country gentleman, country jake, countryman, hayseed, hick, hoosier, hillbilly, jackpine savage, mossback, mountainboomer, pumpkinhusker, railsplitter, cracker, redneck, rube, sharecropper, stump farmer, swamp angel, yahoo, yokel, sodbuster

95. SOMEONE WHO WON'T CHANGE HIS MIND IS: bull-headed, contrary, headstrong, ornery, otsny, owly, pig-headed, set, sot, stubborn, mulish, muley

96. WHEN A GIRL STOPS SEEING A BOY FRIEND SHE IS SAID TO: give him the air, give him the bounce, give him the cold shoulder, give him the mitten, jilt him, kick him, throw him over, turn him down, shoot him down, give him the gate, brush him off, turn him off, break up with him

97. BECOME ILL: be taken sick, get sick, take sick, be taken ill, come down

98. BECOME ILL WITH A COLD: catch a cold, catch cold, get a cold, take cold, take a cold, come down with a cold

99. SICK _____ _____ _____: at his stomach, in his stomach, on his stomach, to his stomach, of his stomach, with his stomach

100. I _____ YOU'RE RIGHT: reckon, guess, figger, figure, suspect, imagine

The preceding vocabulary questionnaire, frequently called a check-list, is only suggestive of what might be asked for in a particular community. Of the hundred items in ten general fields, you may find some questions more interesting and useful to study than others. Furthermore, you may add other words to this list, or you may find other answers to questions listed here.

Let us suppose, however, that you wish to make a vocabulary survey of your community using this checklist. If your school has ample facilities and supplies, you could reproduce all or part of this questionnaire, distribute it to various neighbors, let them fill it out at their leisure, and then have them return it to you for tabulation and analysis.

One last matter of data must be included, however, if the check-list is to be meaningful. The dialectologist needs to know certain things about the people who fill out the checklists. The following questions should be answered if the data are to be interpreted meaningfully.

Let us look for a moment at the personal data sheet. We note that dialectologists think it important to keep a record of the infor-mant's age, sex, race, education, mobility, travel, ancestry, language skills, and occupation. People from the same general area may use different words, and this personal data sheet will help us to find out why. In parts of Michigan, for example, the older generation may still use the term *spider* for what younger informants may call *frying*

Sex_____   Race_____

Have you filled out this same   Age_____ Highest grade level
questionnaire before? Yes____ No____   reached in school_____

State_____ County_____ Town_____

How long have you lived here?_____years

Birthplace_____
                     (town)   (state)

Other towns, states, or nations you have lived in (please give approximate years for
each place)

_____

_____

_____

Have you traveled much outside your native state?_____ (Yes or No)

If so, where?_____

_____

Parents' birthplace (state or nation):

Father_____   Grandfather_____

                                       Grandmother_____

Mother_____   Grandfather_____

                                       Grandmother_____

Do you speak any non-English language?_____ If so, which?_____
                                       (yes or no)

Occupation_____

If retired, **former** occupation_____

If housewife, **husband's** occupation_____

Name (optional)_____

pan. This is an indication of current language change. It is never a surprise to us to hear that our parents' generation did things differently. Nor should we be surprised to note that they use different words.

There are any number of things you may be able to discover by making a vocabulary survey in your community. What you should remember as you gather your data is the principle of constants and variables, a principle familiar to you, no doubt, from mathematics. You may gather your data in any way you wish, but chances are you will not be able to get a representation of all ages, ethnic groups, religions, and occupations of the people in your area, especially if you live in an urban community. A somewhat narrower approach would be easier and more successful, for example:

1. AGE CONTRAST: Collect checklists from three or four people who have lived all their lives in your community. This gives you two constants: the checklist and the native born residents. The most interesting variables will be their age and education along with, of course, their answers. If you select older people and younger people of roughly the same education and social status, chances are that any vocabulary differences will stem from the contrast in ages.

2. EDUCATION CONTRAST: Collect checklists from three or four people who have different educational backgrounds. College graduates, for example, may be contrasted with people who have had less than a high school education. If your informants are of roughly the same age, and if their personal data sheets are otherwise similar, the differences which you note may be attributable to their contrasting educations.

3. DESCRIBE THE LOCAL DIALECT AREA: Collect checklists from three or four people who have lived all their lives in your community. Try to get older, middle-aged, and younger people who have educational backgrounds characteristic of your community (in some parts of our country, for example, college graduates are simply not frequently found). Then note the responses of these informants to some or all of the following questions: 1, 2, 3, 5, 8, 9, 10, 13, 24, 45, 46, 47, 50, 51, 53, 54, 64, 67, 69, 70, 71, 72, 87, 93, 97, 98, 99. For each of these questions there is a response which research has shown to be characteristic of one side of the dialect map shown on page 47 (of course, the term may be used elsewhere too, but not as generally). The following chart will indicate some of the words you may expect to find *in certain parts* of the Northern, Midland, and Southern dialect areas:

Question	Item	Northern	Midland	Southern
1	TO PUT ROOM IN ORDER:		redd up ridd up	
2	PAPER CONTAINER:	bag	sack	sack
3	ON OUTSIDE OF HOUSE:	faucet	spigot spicket hydrant	spigot spicket hydrant
5	CONTAINER:	pail	bucket	bucket
8	METAL UTENSIL: (frying pan common everywhere)	spider	skillet	skillet spider

Question	Item	Northern	Midland	Southern
9	OVER A SINK:	faucet	spigot spicket	spigot spicket
10	BOARDS: (siding common everywhere)	clapboards	weatherboards	
13	DEVICES AT ROOF:	gutters (ENE) eaves spouts eavestroughs	gutters spouting spouts	gutters
24	BABY MOVES:	creeps	crawls	crawls
45	ANIMAL:	skunk	skunk polecat woodspussy woodpussy	polecat
46	ANIMAL: (note: for some people, chipmunk and ground squirrel are two different animals)	chipmunk	ground squirrel	ground squirrel
47	WORM:	angleworm	fish(ing) worm	fish(ing) worm
50	INSECT:	firefly (urban) lightning bug (rural)	lightning bug fire bug	lightning bug
51	INSECT:	(devil's) darning needle sewing bug dragon fly	snake feeder snake doctor dragon fly	snake feeder snake doctor dragon fly mosquito hawk
53	CHERRY:	pit stone	seed stone	seed stone
54	PEACH:	pit stone	seed stone	seed stone
64	DISH:	dessert sauce fruit	dessert fruit	dessert fruit
67	CORN:	corn-on-the-cob green corn sweet corn	corn-on-the-cob sweet corn roasting ears	roasting ears sweet corn
69	TOPS:		greens	greens salad salat
70	CHEESE: (cottage cheese common everywhere)	dutch cheese pot cheese	smear-case	clabber cheese curds
71	CONFECTION:	doughnut fried cake	doughnut	doughnut

Question	Item	Northern	Midland	Southern
72	BREAD:	johnny cake corn bread	corn bread	corn bread corn pone
87	TO CARRY:	armful	armload	armload
93	QUARTER—:	to of	till	till to
97	BECOME ILL:	get sick	take sick	take sick
98	WITH A COLD:	catch a cold	take a cold	take a cold
99	SICK—: (at his stomach common everywhere)	to his stomach	on his stomach in his stomach	

Many of the suggested checklist items have not been surveyed nationally (the automotive terms, for example), and so we cannot show their regional distributions. This should not prevent you from checking them in your own community to discover what term is characteristic there.

4. CONTRAST REGIONAL DIALECTS: Have two natives of your area and two newcomers from other parts of the country fill out all or part of the checklist. Note the contrasts which are evidence of geographical differences. Your conclusions will be more certain if your informants are roughly the same age and have roughly the same educational background. This will help rule out age or education as the cause of the vocabulary difference.

DIFFERENCES IN GRAMMAR

In addition to pronunciation and vocabulary differences in dialects, there are differences which involve matters of grammar. In grammar we include such things as past tenses of verbs, plural nouns, and word order (syntax) patterns. For example, many people use *dived* as the past tense of the verb *dive*. Others use *dove*. Still others use both forms. Likewise, some people say *this is as far as I go*. Others habitually say *this is all the farther I go*. These forms are used by educated and respectable people, and their English is considered equally educated and respectable. If one or two of the above examples sound strange or wrong to you, then you are probably living in an area which uses the alternative form. This does not mean that your way is better or worse—only that it is different.

On the other hand, some variants of grammatical items are used by relatively uneducated people. For the past tense of *dive* they might use the forms *duv* or *div*. For the distance statement they might say *this is the furtherest I go* or *this is the fartherest I go*.

Thus we can see that grammatical items may indicate place of origin or social level. The following chart shows how people in two theoretical areas differ internally, because of social class, and externally, because of where they live.

AREA X		AREA Y	
Speaker	Grammatical item used	Speaker	Grammatical item used
higher social status:	dove	higher social status:	dived
middle social status:	dove	middle social status:	dived
lower social status:	dove, duv	lower social status:	dived, div

Contrary to what some people think, even people of higher social classes do not make the same grammatical choices in different parts of our country. Well-educated natives of Wisconsin tend to say *dove*; their counterparts from Kentucky favor *dived*.

For determining social levels, grammatical choices are as important as pronunciation and vocabulary choices. Regional distributions of grammatical choice, however, are not as clearly marked as other differences. Of particular interest to American fieldworkers are the following items: [1]

1. *Prepositions*
    Trouble comes all _____ once. (to = N, at)
    It's half _____ six. (past, after)
    It's quarter _____ four. (of, to = N, till = M, before, until)
    It's _____ the door. (behind, hindside, in back of, back of)
    He isn't _____. (at home, to home, home)
    It's coming right _____ you. (at, toward, towards)
    Guess who I ran _____. (into, onto, up against, upon, up with, against, again, afoul of = NE, across)
    They named the baby _____ him. (after, for, at, from)
    I fell _____ the horse. (off, off of, offen, off from, from)
    I wonder what he died _____. (of, with, from, for)
    He's sick _____ his stomach. (to = N, at = M, S, of, on = M, in = M, with)
    He came over _____ tell me. (to, for to = SM, S, for = S)
    I want this _____ of that. (instead, stead, in room, in place)

[1] Whenever φ appears, it signifies that nothing is added to the statement. N stands for Northern, M for Midland, S for Southern and NE for New England. For a map of these dialect areas, see page 47.

We're waiting _____ John. (on = M, for)

The old man passed _____. (away, on, out, ϕ)

He did it _____ purpose. (on, a, for, ϕ)

I want _____ the bus. (off = M, to get off)

He was _____ (singing, a-singing) and _____. (laughing, a-laughing)

How big _____ (a, of a) house is it?

2. *Matters of agreement*

Here _____ your pencils. (is, are)

The oats _____ thrashed. (is = M, are = N)

These cabbages _____ (is, are) for sale.

3. *Plural formations*

I have two _____ of shoes. (pair = N, S, pairs = M)

They had forty _____ of apples. (bushel = N, bushels = M)

He has two _____ of butter. (pound = S, pounds = M)

The fence has twenty _____. (posts, post, postis, poss)

He likes to play _____. (horseshoe, horseshoes)

Put your feet in the _____. (stirrup, stirrups)

Let's spray for _____. (moth, moths, mothis)

I bought two _____ of lettuce. (head, heads)

That's a long _____. (way = N, ways = M)

That's a short _____. (way = N, ways = M)

It's nine _____ high. (foot, feet)

We have three _____. (desks, desk, deskis, desses, dess)

4. *Pronouns*

It wasn't _____. (me, I)

This is _____. (yours, yourn)

This is _____. (theirs, theirn)

Are _____ (pl.) coming over? (you, youse, yuz, youns, you-all)

_____ boys are all bad. (those, them, them there)

He's the man _____ owns the car. (that, who, what, which, as, ϕ)

He's the boy _____ father is rich. (whose, that his, that the, his)

"I'm not going!" "_____." (Me either, Me neither, Neither am I, Nor I either, Nor I neither)

It is _____. (I, me)

It is _____. (he, him)

He's going to do it _____. (himself, hisself)

Let them do it _____. (themselves, themself, theirselves, theirself)

I'll go with _____. (ϕ, you)

5. *Adjectives*

The oranges are all _____. (ϕ, gone)

Some berries are _____. (poison, poisonous)

6. *Adverbs*

You can find these almost _____. (anywhere, anywheres, anyplace)

This is _____ I go. (as far as, as fur as, all the farther, all the further, the farthest, the furthest, the fartherest, the furtherest)

7. *Conjunctions*

It seems _____ we'll never win. (as though, like, as if)

I won't go _____ he does. (unless, without, lessen, thouten, douten, less, else)

I like him _____ he's funny. (because, cause, on account of, count, owing to)

Do this _____ I eat lunch. (while, whiles, whilst)

This is not _____ long as that one. (as, so)

8. *Articles*

John is _____ university. (in, in the)

She is _____ hospital. (in, in the)

I have _____ apple. (a, an)

John has _____. (flu, the flu)

Do you have _____? (mumps, the mumps)

9. *Verbs*

Past tense forms:

began, begun, **begin**
blew, blowed
climbed, clim (N), clum (M)
came, come, comed
could, might could (SM, S)
dived, dove (N)
drank, drunk, drinked
did, done
drowned, drownded
ate, et, eat
gave, give (M)
grew, growed
learned, learnt, larnt, larnd
lay, laid
rode, rid
ran, run
saw, seen (M), seed (M), see (N)
sat, set
spoiled, spoilt
swam, swim
threw, throwed
wore, weared
wrote, writ

Past participles:

tore up, **torn up**
wore out, **worn out**
rode (M), ridden
drank, drunk
bit, bitten

Negative:

hadn't ought (N), **ought not**, **oughtn't**, didn't ought

Some of the preceding grammatical choices may seem appropriate to you; others may appear to be undesirable. But in unguarded moments you may find yourself using more than one of the choices. What is particularly interesting to linguists is the fact that many forces contribute to our shift from one variant to another. We will examine these forces in our next chapter.

Grammar Fieldwork

People tend to be much more self-conscious about their use of verb forms, prepositions, pronouns, and so on, than they are about their vocabulary or pronunciation. Consequently, no simple checklist will be given here. However, you can observe the above items in the casual conversations of your acquaintances, in the speech of television actors (especially those who portray Westerners, hillbillies, blue collar urbanites, farmers, well-heeled tycoons, and other special "types"), in the dialogue of novels or short stories, and in the speech of out-of-staters who have recently moved to your community. You must remember, however, that people are very sensitive about their grammar. The good fieldworker is tactful and objective. He does not ridicule the grammar of other areas or other social levels; in fact, he does not even seem to be especially interested in the grammar of his subject's responses. Much of the time he contents himself with getting details of grammar in conversation, without direct questioning.

III. The Reasons for Dialect Differences

In the last chapter we examined regional and social dialect differences in pronunciation, vocabulary, and grammar. It is interesting to observe and record such differences, but the dialectologist is not satisfied to do only this. He is also concerned about the *reasons* for these differences. He assumes that man does not behave in a haphazard, totally independent fashion. Behavior is usually *patterned*, and speech behavior is no exception. In this chapter we will note some of the influences contributing to the *patterned* behavior of American dialects.

1. *The Patterns of Settlement History*

Recently I was driving through the rural Midwest with some friends from California, who noticed things which I had always taken for granted. One Californian, for example, was struck by what he called "little red lollipops" in the front yards of the farmhouses. Later, when he saw another one and called my attention to it, I saw only a red reflector on a stick, used by Indianans as a guide to their driveways at night. My guests were also impressed with poppies growing along the roadside and the quaint country grocery stores with cases of empty soft drink bottles stacked near the front steps. If one grows up in an area in which people usually say "quarter to four," a different but equally common expression, "quarter till four," may seem as strange as the little red lollipops seemed to my friend.

Whether we realize it or not, our language is influenced by the people who settled and established our area. The influence of the early settlers may remain strong for many years; for example, German pronunciations and vocabulary are still found in Grundy County, Illinois; the linguistic effects of the Irish are present on Beaver Island in Lake Michigan; the Dutch influences, in Holland and Grand Rapids, Michigan; and Briticisms, in many American communities which were settled directly from England (such as Albion, Illinois, and New Harmony, Indiana). The first large migration of English people to our country came chiefly from the southeastern counties of England, but there were also some families from Yorkshire, Lancashire, and even the counties farther north. Each of these counties in England has its own local dialects, and the settlers brought these dialects to the New World with them. Later, Ulster Scots, Palatinate Germans, Dutchmen, and others brought features of their own languages or dialects to America, and remnants of these may be clearly seen over one hundred years later.

Sometimes we find a relatively small dialect area surrounded by another, larger one; the former is called a dialect "island." A good example roughly includes parts of northwestern Illinois and southeastern Wisconsin. This lead mining region was settled in the 1850's primarily by people from the Ohio River area, especially Kentucky. Traveling to the region on the Ohio and Mississippi Rivers, these Midland people and some immigrant Cornishmen formed the nucleus of the Lead Region population. To this day, Midland speech predominates here, even though people in all the surrounding areas of both states use Northern speech. Note, too, that this "island" has no regard for political boundaries; it spreads over parts of Illinois, Wisconsin, and Iowa.

Local settlement history, a study often neglected, is vital to the dialectologist as he begins his research. Sometimes he can even supply "missing links" to settlement histories by observing and analyzing speech; for example, a Midwestern area with dialect features usually found in New England is quite likely to have been settled by New Englanders.

The current dialect, although useful, is not a foolproof guide to settlement history, for later layers of settlement may tend to cancel out earlier speech characteristics.

The first American settlers, of course, came from England. At the time of the earliest settlements in Massachusetts, Virginia, Maryland, and Rhode Island, dialect differences in England were even greater than they are today—and today they are still more striking than ours. Speakers of these various dialects crossed the Atlantic Ocean and settled, dialect and all, on the eastern coast of America. The various colonies of the New World found communication very difficult, and the mixed dialects of English settlers who inhabited each colony gradually became distinctive in themselves. The infrequent visits from "outsiders," the lack of safe and efficient transportation methods, and the tendency of each colony to act as a social unit did much to make their dialects distinctive. To this day the eastern coast of our country has smaller and more clearly defined dialect areas than does almost any region to the west.

2. *Patterns of Population Shift*

Ask almost anyone what the dialects of America are, and you probably will be told that they are Southern, Eastern, and General American (meaning Midwestern and Western). Even though some textbooks encourage this notion, Americans simply are not divided that neatly. Nor are regional dialects organized along state lines, as we have already seen. There is simply no such thing as a single New York, Ohio, or Florida dialect; the dialects of these and other states are formed along the lines of population shift. Nor do national borders necessarily mark dialect (or, for that matter, language) differences. The U.S.-Canadian border has been crossed many times by immigrants from both nations. One interesting example of this movement occurred during the Civil War when groups of New Englanders, hoping to avoid conscription, felt the urge to move to New Brunswick. Such immigrants were referred to as *Skedaddlers*, and to this day one of their settlements is known locally as Skedaddlers Ridge.

Since the American population shift generally has been from east to west, dialect boundaries are more apt to run horizontally than vertically. People from, say, western New York who moved to Michigan, Wisconsin, northern Illinois, and northern Ohio took their western New York dialect with them.

Population shift is affected by the opening of new travel routes, by the invention of new means of transportation, by the development of industry, and by other aspects of American history. And speech patterns are thus moved and changed. For instance, the steamboat ushered in a whole new concept of American migration, allowing New Englanders and the more recent immigrants to move west across the Great Lakes.

The effects of population shift caused by industrialization can be seen in cities like Akron, Ohio. This area was settled later than most urban areas of Ohio because it is located on a high spot (Summit County) just south of the general migration route through Cleveland and just north of the route through Columbus. When the rubber industry began to develop, Akron drew thousands of laborers from the handiest source of labor; southern Ohio, West Virginia, and Kentucky. The tremendous in-pouring of Midlanders has had such a noticeable effect on the speech of Akronites that, despite its Northern location, Akron might well be considered part of the Midland speech area. The migration of Midlanders, especially West Virginians, in the past twenty years is also clearly evident in the

Cleveland area, where it is estimated that Cuyahoga County has received 150,000 migrants from other states since World War II. Professor Raven I. McDavid, Jr., of the University of Chicago has observed that Kentucky and West Virginia, like western New England in our country's earlier days, have the two qualities necessary for emigration: a high fertility in the population and a low fertility in the soil.

Along with mention of the shift of population, we must also note the development of urban prestige. Cities like New York, Philadelphia, New Orleans, and San Francisco have acquired a certain prestige and have become culturally influential. Of course, no one city dominates American culture or American speech; a combination of factors causes Americans to use regional forms rather than a "national" pattern of speech.

One such factor is found in the very size of our country. It is simply too large for one city to develop a network of influence over every other city. If such an influence had ever existed, today we would most likely be imitating the speech of New York City, Boston, Philadelphia, Washington, D. C., or some other city significant in our nation's history.

Democracy also affects the thinking of Americans. If we should be told suddenly that we should pattern our speech, dress, buying habits, religion, and political views after those of Cedar Rapids, Iowa, most of us would react violently. Why Cedar Rapids? The spirit of American regionalism may be seen in people from almost any area of the country. The most traditional example might be a Texan, whose loyalty is notorious. But it can also be seen in the regional loyalty of the natives of Washington State, the Great Lakes area, and New England. This feeling is encouraged by local businessmen whose constant plea is "Buy local products," and by the pressures of family life which cause people to take local jobs rather than to move to some other part of the country.

As a result of this loyalty, various urban areas become focal points in the culture, including the dialect, of a given area. Pronunciations, words, and even grammatical choices of a city are often copied, consciously or subconsciously, by people around it. The influence of Chicago speech patterns can be clearly seen as far west as Wheaton, Illinois (twenty-five miles from Chicago), for example, where such characteristic Chicago words as *prairie* (for vacant lot) and *clout* (political influence) are known. The spread of the Minneapolis influence into Wisconsin was recently noted by Frederic G. Cassidy, who observed that the Minneapolis term *rubber-binder* (for rubber band) was gaining across the state line. On the other hand, the exact influence of an urban area is difficult to judge. The mere presence of a word or pronunciation in the city and its surrounding area does not guarantee that the primary influence came from the city. The flat farm land west of Chicago was actually settled before that city began its phenomenal growth, and it is difficult to sort out the influences of both areas. William Labov has recently observed that lower income New York City residents often ridicule their own speech. The pronunciations *dis* and *dese* (for *this* and *these*) are thought of as characteristic of lower social levels and are not highly valued.

More recent immigration patterns also have had their influence on American English. There can be little doubt about the impact of foreign languages in the past century. The influence of German settlers on the vocabulary and syntax of certain parts of Pennsylvania has long been recognized; likewise, one can easily find Polish terms in Detroit, Hungarian in Cleveland, and Spanish in Los Angeles. New people bring new customs and, quite frequently, new ways of expressing them. Other aspects of American history have also contributed to the dialect mixtures of the present day. Many of our earlier settlements in the Rocky Mountains, for example, dissolved along with the mines which attracted the settlers in the first place. Similarly, those early eastern Coloradans who tried the wrong farming techniques soon moved to other parts, taking their dialect heritage with them and leaving the dust bowl behind.

3. *Patterns of Physical Geography*

Today we are seldom hindered in our travels by physical barriers such as rivers, deserts, or mountains. Bridge building, improved water travel, earthmoving techniques, and air transportation have removed most of the barriers which hampered communications and population shift in the last century. Consequently, dialect differences which are found on opposite sides of a river, a mountain range, or a desert were probably established many years ago. In more recently settled areas we find the influences of physical geography less important; however, there are some recent examples of cultural and linguistic isolation. Until about forty years ago river transportation was almost the only way for residents of Calhoun County, Illinois, to travel outside the county to Alton, Illinois, for a distance of about one hundred miles. Likewise Leslie County, Kentucky, had only one paved road as recently as ten years ago. This type of isolation can be seen today in parts of eastern Kentucky and southern Virginia, and more examples might be found in many other states.

In the East, rivers, mostly because they were early physical barriers, are rather clear markers of dialect areas. The Connecticut River still separates *pahk the cah* from *park the car*. As far west as Illinois, the prairie south of the Rock River and north of the Illinois River provided easy access for the settlement of Yankees who came to Illinois across the Great Lakes and Midlanders who came north by way of the Mississippi and Illinois Rivers. Today this prairie area contains a mixture of Northern and Midland dialects. West of the Mississippi, however, geographical barriers are seldom important, since settlement often developed along with the railroad or even followed it, instead of being determined by water routes and boundaries.

Fieldwork in Historical Background and Social Structure

One of the first things a dialectologist does in his investigation of a given area is to find out as much as he can about its settlement history. Sometimes he can discover a little from published histories of the city or state. In some parts of the country, county histories are available through local libraries or county historical societies. State historical societies may provide useful information, often through an official publication or journal. A good beginning point for a class studying dialects, therefore, is the available historical material. Teacher and students alike might want to go beyond the school library's collection to that of the local, county, or state historical society.

The dialectologist is interested in the basic patterns of settlement history, population shift, physical geography, and social structure. Of these patterns, the social structure may be the most difficult to determine. An investigation of the speech of your area, along with the education, the occupation, and the age of your informants, may tell you as much about social structure as any kind of information can. Try to answer these questions:

1. *Where did the people who settled this area come from?*

This information is sometimes stated directly in state or county histories, but more often we must guess, using maps which show population density at different times. For example, some of the earliest settlers in Illinois came to the southern part of the state. This suggests that they came from neighboring southern areas. See such standard references as Charles O. Paullin and John K. Wright, *Atlas of the Historical Geography of the United States*

(Washington and New York: Carnegie Institution of Washington and the American Geographical Society of New York, 1932), or the U. S. Census publications.

2. *How did they come?*

If your area is on or near a river, a canal, the Great Lakes, an early national highway, a valley pass through a mountain range, or a sea coast, you can expect to find traces of the speech of people who traveled these routes. Early southern settlements in Illinois, for example, point to migrations from Kentucky and Tennessee via the Ohio and Mississippi Rivers. The end of the Black Hawk War, the invention of the steamboat, and the financial depression of 1831–1840 all facilitated a second period of Illinois settlement, this time by Yankees. Most of these western New England settlers came by way of the Great Lakes and settled in the northeast corner of the state—largely north of the Illinois River. Some New Englanders went on south and west into easily reached prairie farming areas such as Bureau, Henry, Knox, and Stark Counties. Midlanders settled near rivers and avoided the prairie because they were more interested in hunting and trapping than in farming.

3. *What changes in population have taken place since original settlement?*

Frequently this question may be answered by tracing the economic history of the area. Have recent industrial developments attracted migrant laborers? The construction of the Chrysler Motors plant at Hudson, Ohio, for example, has had a profound effect on the former New England character of that community.

Sometimes a simple examination of U. S. Census statistics will vividly illustrate such things as an increase in the Negro population of a Northern urban center, a decrease in upper and middle income professional people in a particular area, an increase or decrease of county population (from 1950 to 1960 DuPage County, Illinois, increased its population by 102.8 percent as compared to the total state of Illinois increase of 15.7 percent), or the increase of Negroes of professional status—as in Washington, D. C., in recent years.

The following map will give a rough idea of what can be discovered about population mobility within an American city. In the city of Detroit, we can observe definite patterns of group mobility. The movement of a Negro from Inner City to Middle City may show his climb in socioeconomic status; research now indicates that this climb is also reflected in his pronunciation, vocabulary, and grammar.

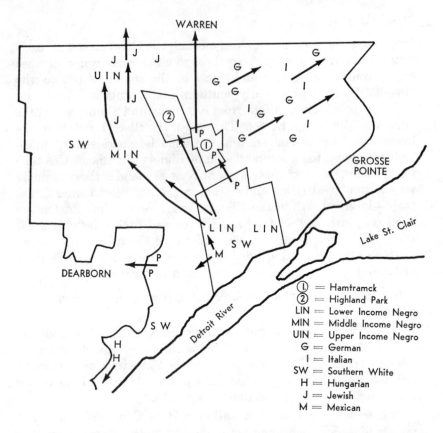

Recent white migrants from Southern states, particularly from Appalachia, tend to settle in three parts of the city, as the map indicates, or in the less affluent suburban areas where they have small farms. The Detroit Polish population likewise moves in a fairly well-established pattern, although it is certainly less restricted than that of the Negro or, more interestingly perhaps, the Mexican. Mexican immigrants, as the map indicates, have a much shorter mobility pattern—at least so far.

These factors, usually seen as the special property of history or social studies courses, are also significant in the study of American English. Our language, after all, reflects our history, geography, and social contacts. American education is finally showing awareness of the fact that we must study the speech of people who are prevented by any reason—economics, race, religion, or national background—from reaching the success they are capable of. And studying the speech of a particular group will help us understand and appreciate the group itself. Many Northerners need to learn that Southern or Midland speech is not necessarily substandard; many Southerners and Mid-landers need to learn that a Northern speaker is not just "conceited." Many need to learn that climate, thickness of lips, or skin color have absolutely nothing to do with speech.

Specific problems that arise accidentally can sometimes be traced to language. White citizens in Las Vegas, Nevada, only recently learned that Negroes in that city prefer to be called "Negroes," not "colored people." This sort of situation can cause one group to feel uncomfortable or even insulted, though the other group had no idea their choice of words was offensive.

The study of speech, therefore has two potential benefits:

1. to the person whose speech keeps him from the success he wants—so that he can learn acceptable forms.
2. to the person who has already learned at least some acceptable forms—so that he will not scorn acceptable speech from other parts of the country, from other social levels, or from other races.

IV. American Dialects Today

Finding the Dialect Areas of American English

Dialectologists record on maps the pronunciations, words, and grammatical forms which they find in an area. These items are represented by various symbols. Map 1, a map of several Eastern states,

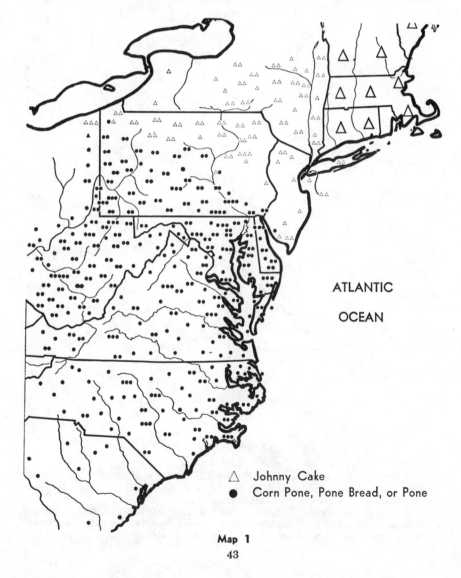

ATLANTIC

OCEAN

△ Johnny Cake
● Corn Pone, Pone Bread, or Pone

Map 1

illustrates this procedure.[1] The circles indicate the communities in-
vestigated. As the legend explains, informants represented by circles
say either *corn pone, pone bread,* or *pone.* Informants from the other
communities (triangles) say *johnnycake.* Map 2 shows the distribution of the two ways the verb *dive* is used in the past tense in northern
Illinois.[2]

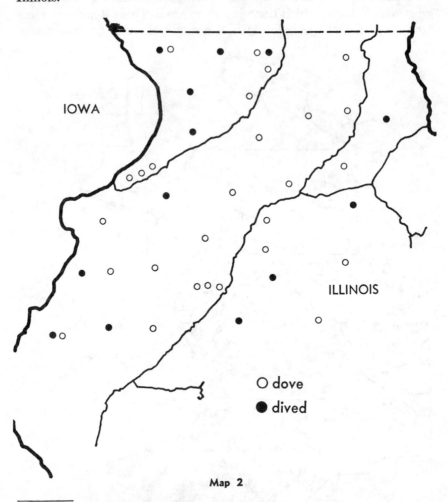

Map 2

---

[1] Adapted from Hans Kurath, *A Word Geography of the Eastern United
States* (Ann Arbor: University of Michigan Press, 1949), Figure 116; used
by permission of University of Michigan Press.

[2] Adapted from Roger W. Shuy, "The Northern-Midland Dialect Boundary
in Illinois," publication of the American Dialect Society, No. 38, (November
1962), 50; used by permission of the American Dialect Society.

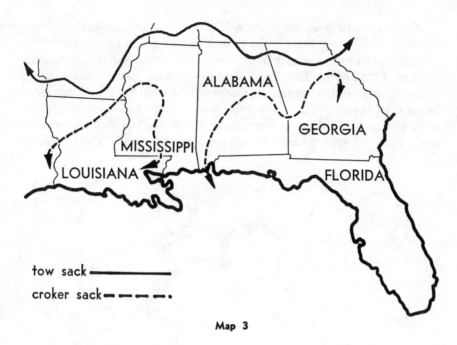

tow sack ─────────
croker sack ──────

Map 3

Eastern Limits
frijoles ─────────
pilón ──────────

Map 4

Once a number of such maps has been made, the dialectologist looks for similar patterns. Where he finds that one pronunciation or word is used almost entirely in one area, he draws a line which encloses the use of that item. This line, called an isogloss, marks the boundary of the pronunciation, word, or grammatical form. Such isoglosses can be seen in Map 3,[3] where the solid line indicates how far south the term *tow sack* (burlap bag) extends. The dotted line shows how far north the term *croker sack* (burlap bag) can be found. The arrows at

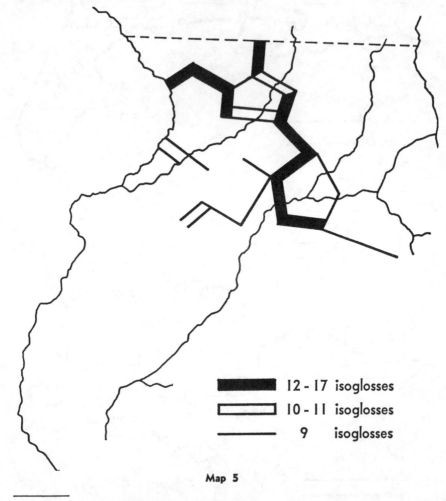

12 - 17 isoglosses
10 - 11 isoglosses
9   isoglosses

Map 5

[3] Adapted from Gordon R. Wood, "Dialect Contours in the Southern States," *American Speech* (December 1963), p. 244; used by permission of Columbia University Press, 2960 Broadway, New York, N.Y. 10027.

the end of each line point toward the areas enclosed by them. Isoglosses marking the distribution of *frijoles* (pinto beans) and *pilón* (something extra) in Texas are found in Map 4.[4] Examining these isoglosses, the dialectologist finds patterns of their direction. He determines whether or not several isoglosses are found in the same place. One way to do this is to draw several isoglosses on the same map and see where they coincide. Map 5 shows how this technique was carried out in northern Illinois. The dark line symbolizes areas where twelve to seventeen isoglosses pattern identically. The double line describes areas where ten or eleven isoglosses converge. The single line stands for nine isoglosses in the same area.

Using such techniques, then, American dialect geographers have tried to find the major and minor dialect areas of our country. Map 6 shows some of the major boundaries that have been established so far, although a great deal of work remains to be done.

Map 6

---

[4] Adapted from E. Bagby Atwood, *The Regional Vocabulary of Texas* (Austin: University of Texas Press, 1962), p. 80; used by permission of University of Texas Press.

V. The Influence of Foreign Languages on American Dialects

Place Names

A list of place names for almost any state will give clues about its history and social structure. For example, the following cities and towns are all in Michigan:

Spring Arbor	Ann Arbor	Atlanta
New Boston	Nashville	Grosse Isle
L'Anse	Au Gres	Onondaga
Detroit	Charlotte	Ithaca
Kalamazoo	Wenona Beach	St. Johns
Vanderbilt	Holland	Grand Ledge
Hudson	Utica	Union Pier
St. Louis	St. Claire	Vermontville
Port Austin	Grand Haven	Grosse Pointe
Glen Arbor	Port Huron	Graafschap
New Baltimore	Brooklyn	Troy
Charlevoix	De Tour	St. Joseph
Presque Isle	Sebewaing	Akron
Quanicassee	Zeeland	Eau Claire
Vandercook	New Buffalo	Watervliet
Rochester	St. Ignace	Richmondville
St. Charles	Grand Rapids	Marlette
Saugatuck	Portland	Marquette
	Sandusky	Grandville

Listed as they are above, the place names are not as revealing of settlement history as the following rearranged list:

1. Spring Arbor
   Glen Arbor
   Ann Arbor

2. New Boston
   New Baltimore
   Nashville
   Brooklyn
   Sandusky
   Atlanta
   Vermontville
   Akron
   Richmondville

3. L'Anse
   Detroit
   Charlevoix
   Presque Isle
   Au Gres
   Charlotte
   De Tour
   Grosse Isle
   Grosse Pointe
   Eau Claire
   Marlette
   Marquette

4. Kalamazoo
   Quanicassee
   Wenona Beach
   Sebewaing
   Onondaga
   Saugatuck

5. Vanderbilt
   Vandercook
   Holland
   Zeeland
   Graafshap
   Watervliet

6. Hudson	7. St. Louis	8. Grand Haven
Rochester	St. Charles	Grand Rapids
Utica	St. Claire	Grand Ledge
New Buffalo	St. Ignace	Grandville
Ithaca	St. Johns	
Akron	St. Joseph	9. Port Austin
Troy		Port Huron
		Portland
		Union Pier

We can see quite easily that the place names suggest settlement history and geography and, to a certain extent, the economy and religion of the area. The influence of the French in Michigan can be seen from the place names in Group 3. Likewise, the Dutch names of Group 5 point to some significant Dutch settlements.

Group 2 contains a geographical mixture of place names which *may* have been based on settlement history. We cannot always be sure of these matters, however, as some early records may reveal. For example, the city of Vermont, Illinois, was named by the only Northern member of the community, who gave two jugs of whiskey for the right to name the town. A bit clearer is the relationship of the names of Group 6 to Michigan settlement history. All of these names, with the possible exception of Akron, derive from New York State locations. It is difficult to tell whether Akron bears its debt to Ohio or New York. Indian languages play a prominent part in place names in most of our states. Michigan's contribution is clearly evident in Group 4.

Groups 1, 7, 8, and 9 show different aspects of the life of Michigan. The presence of *arbor* in three place names points to an aspect of the area's topography (for arbor means "grove" in this case), the *Saint* names show early French Catholic influence, and the names in Groups 8 and 9 indicate the presence of a river (the Grand River) and commercial lake harbors.

Vocabulary

Many of the names of everyday objects which we take for granted as native English are, in reality, borrowings from other tongues. The history of the English language clearly parallels the history of the people who influenced it. It is not surprising to see French influence stemming from the Norman Conquest, Scandinavian influences during the tenth century, and Latin borrowings during the sixteenth, seventeenth, and eighteenth centuries, during the rebirth of interest in classical times.

But what about more recent influences from foreign languages? We must recognize our debt to American Indian languages for such words as *hickory, moccasin, raccoon, skunk, moose, toboggan,* and many others which entered American English because of the colonists' need to describe things that were unfamiliar to them. What words the colonists adopted depended of course on where they were. For example, the borrowings from Ojibwa are more commonly found in areas where the Ojibwa lived. To this day *chipmunk,* a borrowing from Algonquian, is found in Northern dialect areas where Ojibwa and other Algonquians dominated, in contrast to (or in addition to) *ground squirrel,* which is used by Midlanders. Likewise, *skunk,* of Algonquian origins, predominates in Northern speech, while *polecat* is more often used in some other parts of the country. Nor is it surprising to find the term borrowed from Peguots, *quahog* (a hard clam), in coastal New England but not in the coastal South.

The languages of other colonizing nations also contributed to the English of the New World. Thus from the Dutch we received cherry *pit, boss, snoop, stoop, cookie, sugar bush,* and *waffle.* Even *Santa Claus* is attributable to the Dutch settlers of the New York region. *Boss, snoop, cookie,* and *waffle* have become so well assimilated by Americans that they are considered English. But cherry *pit* and peach *pit* still dominate in Northern dialect areas, while cherry *seed* and peach *seed* are used by many Midland and Southern speakers. Likewise the word *stoop* (for front steps in cities, or porch in rural areas) is found more commonly in the Northern dialect areas to which the New York Dutch (or those who had lived among them) migrated. The Dutch word for wilderness, *bossch,* led to *sugar bush* (meaning maple grove), another term which spread west from the Hudson Valley and is considered dialectal.

Negro slaves in eighteenth century America were, of course, of inferior social status. It is not surprising, therefore, that the various languages of the slaves had comparatively little influence on American vocabulary, although there are a few examples. The Kimbundu word for peanut, *nguba,* is retained as *goober* in America, particularly in the South. The Banbara word *kuta* became *cooter* (a synonym for *turtle*) in American English. It is also found primarily in the South, as Marjorie Kinnans Rawlings' novel set in north Florida, *The Yearling,* bears evidence. Other African borrowings include *gumbo, banjo, zombi, hoodoo,* and *voodoo.*

Spanish too has had an influence on the American English vocabulary, but not extensively until the nineteenth century. As the colonists moved farther south and west, it was inevitable that they should come in contact with Spanish speakers. Such words as *mosquito, stevedore,* and *Negro* were borrowed in early colonial days. The Westward movement, the Gold Rush, the Spanish-American War, and the popularization of "the Western" in movies and on television have brought *lasso, siesta, ranch, corral, patio, mustang, canyon,* and *burro* into American English. For a detailed examination of the presence of Spanish words in Texas, Oklahoma, New Mexico, Arkansas, and Louisiana today, the student should examine E. Bagley Atwood's *The Regional Vocabulary of Texas.* Among the words cited by Atwood are

toro	(bull)
resaca	(body of water)
hacienda	(ranching establishment)
arroyo	(dry creek)
frijoles	(pinto beans)—see Map 4, p. 45
mesa	(high, flat land)
remuda	(group of saddle horses)
morral	(feed bag)
pilón	(an extra gift accompanying a purchase)

The recent influences of French on American English vocabulary are largely from the bayou country of southwestern Louisiana, where French is still spoken by half a million people. This area, settled originally by displaced French settlers (called Acadians) from Nova Scotia in the eighteenth century, abounds with French borrowings. Atwood's *The Regional Vocabulary of Texas* points out that many French words are in common use in parts of Louisiana and Texas today, particularly in the rural areas. Among these words are

banquette	(sidewalk)
lagniappe	(an extra gift accompanying a purchase)
cush-cush	(a corn meal preparation)
pirogue	(boat used on a river)
armoire	(wardrobe with drawers)
bayou	(running stream)
praline	(pecan candy)
la!	(command to a cow to make her stand still)

Some French words have also been borrowed from Canadian French, often directly, including *chowder,* to *sashay, batteau, levee, rapids, portage,* and *prairie.* Furthermore, American colonists frequently used the French suffix *-ville* for place names, even though it was not common in England.

It was mid-nineteenth century before German vocabulary borrowings were very extensive. It may seem strange, perhaps, that a Germanic language should later be influenced by German—but such is the fate of a borrowing tongue; most Americans know and use the words *kindergarten, dunk, delicatessen, ouch, sauerkraut, loafer,* and *dumb,* all of which are so embedded in our speech that we do not think of them as dialect terms. In regions heavily settled by Germans (including Pennsylvania and Wisconsin and much of the urban Midwest), many German words with less national distributions are still used. Cottage cheese may be called *smear–case,* a bag may be called a *toot,* and dried apples may be referred to as *snits.* Descendants of the German settlers along the Mississippi River near Kaskaskia, Illinois, for example, still use the term *vipkenbrot* to refer to headcheese and residents of German origin in Philadelphia use *wurst* to refer to a kind of luncheon meat. All of these, and many others, may be considered dialect terms via German and are characteristic of German settlement history.

American English has borrowed less actively from other languages. When a word is borrowed, it is usually a term for which there is no English equivalent. Consequently, we have borrowed many names for foreign foods and eating customs from the Italian (*spaghetti, pizza,* and *macaroni*), Chinese (*chow mein*), Yiddish (*gefilte fish, bagel,* and *blintz*), and Swedish (*smorgasbord, lingnon,* and *lefse*). Some of these terms became widely used, while others still show the nationality of their users. In Minnesota and neighboring states, one may well expect to hear Scandinavian words which are not found elsewhere to any extent.

Fieldwork in Foreign Language Influences on American English

1. *Foreign Origins in Place Names*

Using a roadmap or atlas of your county or state, note the place names which show the influence of French, Indian, Dutch, Scandinavian, Spanish, or German origins. Other language backgrounds may also be noted, but the above languages are most common in American place names. You may wish to get help from teachers of French, Spanish, or German, or you may use standard reference works on history, language, or geography. Your librarian will be able to guide your research in this matter. The economy, geography, politics, and social structure of an area may also be revealed in the place names of a state; for example, Temperance, Michigan, may reflect the mid-nineteenth century period of American liquor legislation.

2. Foreign Origins in Vocabulary

To study foreign borrowings in your area, try the following check-list in your community. The national origin of your informant may tell a great deal about his vocabulary, and vice versa.

A CHECKLIST OF VOCABULARY

DIRECTIONS

1. Please put a check in the appropriate column or columns.
2. If the word you ordinarily use is not listed, please write it in the space provided.
3. If you never use any word in the group and if you have never heard it, do not mark the word.

Definition	Item	I use this term.	I have heard this but I do not use it.	I heard it in _____ (town or state)	This is a foreign word.
1. In the center of a cherry	pit				
	seed				
	stone				
2. Small squirrel-like animal	chipmunk				
	ground squirrel				
3. Common round clam	quahog				
	clam				
4. Porch with roof	piazza				
	porch				
	stoop				
5. Animal with bad odor	skunk				
	polecat				
6. Place where maple syrup is produced	maple grove				
	sugar bush				
7. A kind of bean	pinto bean				
	frijoles				
8. Extra gift accompanying a purchase	pilón				
	lagniappe				
9. Pecan candy	pecan praline				
	pecan patty				

Item	I use this term.	I have heard this but I do not use it.	I heard it in _____ (town or state)	This is a foreign word.
10. Running stream				
branch				
creek				
run				
bayou				
11. Place to walk				
sidewalk				
banquette				
12. Body of water				
lake				
resaca				
13. Horses eat from it				
feed bag				
morral				
14. A type of topography				
mesa				
high, flat land				
15. Male cow				
bull				
toro				
16. A type of berry				
lingnon				
17. A kind of pastry				
kolachi				
18. Pieces of dried apple				
dried apple				
snits				
19. Type of cheese				
cottage cheese				
smear–case				
20. Movable place to hang clothes				
closet				
armoire				
wardrobe				
21. Meat used in sandwiches				
luncheon meat				
wurst				

The preceding questionnaire, like the longer vocabulary check-list of Chapter II, may serve as a base to which other questions may be added. Do not be alarmed if your informants are not familiar with some of the terms; it may be that only a few of these foreign borrowings are known in your area. You will also need more information about your informants:

Sex_____ Race_____ Age_____

What nationality were your ancestors?_____

Where do you live at present?_____

How long have you lived there?_____

Where were you born?_____

Other towns, states, or nations in which you have lived (please give approximate years for each place):

_____

_____

_____

_____

VI. The Use of Dialects in Literature

Since literature records the struggles of individual men in social situations, many authors knowingly or unknowingly use their knowledge of varieties of English as a literary device. We might ask, "How do we know that a character is educated or uneducated, Texan or Bostonian?" Since the technique of the good writer is to *show* rather than to *tell*, we frequently are *shown* the education, social status, regional background, and culture of a character by his speech.

As a literary device, however, the indication of his dialect may be distorted for effect, just as political cartoonists exaggerate the facial features of people in the news, to make them quickly recognizable. In literature, the author is handicapped in the number of speeches a character can make, for, after all, a novel must be reasonably short; therefore, he must identify his characters quickly and unmistakably if possible.

The author is further handicapped by our conventional alphabet. The phonetic symbols mentioned in Chapter II are not available to him. He must let us know, somehow, that the character is saying [kæʊ] instead of [kɑʊ] for the word *cow*. The writer may choose to spell it *cauw* or *cayow* or a number of other possible ways.

A third handicap faced by many authors is their lack of understanding of other, and even their own, dialects. Most of us are shocked when we hear our own voices on a tape recorder and when we see ourselves in home movies. And who among us has ever really been pleased with the proofs from his photographer? An author may be more sensitive to the "stuff" of life, but he is almost as likely as the next person to be unaware of the dialects of his home area.

The author of a short story or novel is, therefore, limited by his alphabet, by his nearness to his own dialect, and by the nature of his task. He must concentrate on plot, theme, unity, and many other literary matters. If he can accomplish the desired characterization by means of dialect, he may try to do so. For various reasons, many authors do not.

Writers who *do* attempt to represent regional or social dialects in literary dialogue frequently employ eye-dialect. This form of dialect is not really dialect at all, for it may not represent a variant pronunciation. Instead, it suggests an illiterate or relatively uneducated character by using spelling errors. *Can*, for example, may be spelled *kin*. The latter spelling, while it suggests a substandard pronunciation, is actually very close to the way many educated speakers of standard English say the word under certain circumstances. Other respellings which suggest substandard speech but which really represent rather standard pronunciations are *wuz* for *was*, *sez* for *says*, *duz* for *does*, *ah'll* for *I'll* (an educated pronunciation in a large portion of the country), and *goin'* for *going* (along with *gonna* for *going to*). By using these features of eye-dialect, the fiction writer may cause his readers to react as though the characters were, indeed, users of substandard English. If this reaction was intended, he is a successful writer. He may also successfully indicate casual speech in this way. In terms of actual dialect, however, he has said very little. Pronunciations represented through the English spelling system are tricky. They may represent a regional or social dialect, but frequently they indicate just that the character is less than well educated. And what could be more natural? Spelling, unlike pronunciation, has become fairly standardized so that deviation from standard spelling clearly indicates a poor education. The reader sees the misspelled word, associates it with the character, and understands what the author is saying about him.

On the other hand, spellings which accurately represent regional varieties or social levels may be found in literature. A Northern farmer who says *bekuz* (for *because*) well exemplifies speakers from the northern Midwest. Two of the eye-dialect spellings may turn out to be accurate regional or social representation: *ah'll* is more likely to be used by Midland or Southern speakers of all education groups, and *goin'* tends to be characteristic of the less educated (but it also has some currency among the more assured educated classes).

Vocabulary is much easier to use as dialect indicator if the author has control of the dialect he is representing. Any of the items mentioned in the vocabulary section of Chapter II could be illustrations; my own speech contains a mixture of Northern and Midland vocabulary, since I come from a transition area. If someone from my home area were to be represented in fiction, he might well use Midland words like *bucket* and *spigot* along with Northern words like *bag*, *chipmunk*, and *armful*.

Grammatical forms, as mentioned earlier, have more to do with social than regional dialects. But Northern characters in literature may be expected to say *dove* (rather than *dived*), *hadn't ought*, and *sick to the stomach*. Certain Midlanders might well say *quarter till*, *a long ways*, and *I want off.* Some Southerners might say *I might could, I taken it*, and *the sun riz.*

It is possible to find examples of American regional and social dialects in many short stories, novels, and plays. The short stories of Jesse Stuart illustrate the dialect of eastern Kentucky. Joel Chandler Harris's Uncle Remus stories portray the older generation Piedmont Negro. Ring Lardner's novels are full of the middle class and folk speech of the Midwest. Mark Twain's novels and short stories illustrate the dialects of Missouri and other Mississippi River territory to the south (see his prefatory note to *Huckleberry Finn*). Patterson Greene's play, *Papa Is All*, uses the speech of the Pennsylvania Dutch.

Fieldwork in Dialects in Literature

1. Compare a dialogue sequence in *The Yearling* or *Hie to the Hunters* with one in *The Catcher in the Rye* or *It's All Right, Cat!* Note the differences between back country and urban spoken language. Are the vocabulary differences related to different times, different needs, and different environments?[1]

2. Discover some of the influences of Norwegian on American English by reading John Van Druten's play, *I Remember Mama.* You may do the same thing with Ole Rölvaag's *Giants in the Earth* and *Peder Victorious* as well as Martha Ostenso's *The Mad Carews.* Look up the Norwegianisms in a Norwegian-English dictionary.

3. Make a list of Pennsylvania Dutch words and phrases (especially in word order) found in Elsie Singmaster's short story "The Belsnickel" and in Patterson Greene's play *Papa Is All*.

4. Note the Nebraska vocabulary found in the novels of Willa Cather (*O Pioneers!* and *My Antonia*, for example). On the basis of the word lists given in Chapter II, would you call Nebraska a Northern or Midland dialect area?

5. Observe the influences of Yiddish on American English in the short stories of Arthur Kober ("That Man Is Here Again" and "Bella, Bella Kissed a Fella," for example) and in the novels of Leo Rosten (*The Education of Hyman Kaplan*), Bernard Malamud (*The Natural*), and Saul Bellow (*Seize the Day* and *Herzog*).[2]

---

[1] Suggested by Evelyn Gott of Westport, Connecticut.

[2] Suggested by Robert Hanson of Shaker Heights, Ohio.

6. Collect examples of Chicago Irishisms in the novels of Finley P. Dunne (*Mr. Dooley Says* and other "Mr. Dooley" novels) and James T. Farrell (*Studs Lonigan*).

7. Note east Tennessee vocabulary and syntax in the novels of Mary Murfree (*In the Tennessee Mountains* and *The Prophet of the Great Smoky Mountains*) and in the collections of short stories by Mildred Haun (*That Hawk's Done Gone*).

8. Observe the different dialects found in Mark Twain's *Huckleberry Finn*. Do Huck and Jim speak a prestige dialect? Does the fact that Twain realistically describes the speech of Negro slaves affect his argument against slavery and racial discrimination?

9. Note the grammatical structure and vocabulary of Quaker speech as you observe it in the short stories of Jessamyn West ("The Battle of Finney's Ford") and Mabel Hunt ("Little Girl with Seven Names"). Pay particular attention to the second person personal pronouns and third person singular present tense verb forms. In Albert C. Baugh's *A History of the English Language*, look up the history of these forms, noting especially the influence of George Fox and the Quaker movement.

10. Examine Irene Hunt's short story "Across Five Aprils" for its use of eye–dialect. Assuming that the author wants us to note the maturity of Jethro and the simple-minded weakness of Eb, how does her use of eye–dialect contribute to this purpose? Note especially the words fer (for), git (get), comfert (comfort), jest (just), fergit (forget), yore (your), stummick (stomach), ner (nor), and kin (can). Who uses them? Who does not? Should an author have only the "bad guys" use dialect?

VII. Further Work in Dialectology

As you may suspect, American dialectology is becoming both more complex and more interesting. Twenty or thirty years ago dialect geographers were mainly concerned with relating current pronunciations, vocabulary, and grammar to settlement history and geography. In the sixties, the problems of urban living have attracted attention, including social dialects and styles which need to be learned and used to meet different situations. We need more precise information about the dialects which set one social group apart from another. What specific linguistic changes must a person make when he moves from one group to another? Even now studies on these and other problems are being carried on in New York, Chicago, Detroit, Washington, D.C., and several other cities.

Although we have concentrated on the effects of age and geography on dialects, social status and intended style are also important. The following chart illustrates the situation, although it is greatly oversimplified here. (One accurate chart would probably be impossible, because of its size and complexity!)

Social dialects are subcategories of regional dialects. One observation which has been made about them is that, comparing dialects of well-educated speakers of different areas, pronunciation varies more than grammar does. We do not yet have enough data to make many such statements about social dialects; however, we must remember that any comparison between regional dialects should be made on the same social level. It would be unfair and confusing to compare the speech of an educated Kentuckian with that of an uneducated New Yorker, or vice versa. Yet many educated speakers make just this mistake when they think of the dialects of other areas.

Styles are subcategories of an individual's speech, used according to the situation he is in. His deliberative style (found, perhaps, in a serious classroom discussion) may differ from his casual style (used with friends), his intimate style (used between brothers, for example), or his formal style (used in speech class). Whether a response is one word or a long explanation may also cause a change in style. Emotions also matter; think of the speech of any one person, excited or calm. What differences are there in his choice of words, pronunciation, and grammar? Here again it is obvious that no one chart could possibly show the many subcategories of the English

63

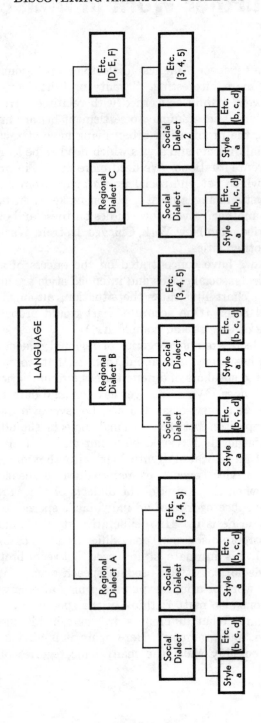

language. As in any field of knowledge, the more answers we find, the more new questions appear.

The addition of social and stylistic variations to those of age and geography and history makes language study immensely complicated. At the same time, it has practical uses for every speaker. First, we can understand why our dialects identify us—and we can change both our speech and the resulting identification if we wish. Second, and even more important, we can recognize the dialects of others for what they are: results of forces over which they have little control. Instead of reacting with contempt or confusion, we can begin to appreciate the richness of variety in the English language.

There are many additional books and articles about dialects that you might want to read, including the following:

Allen, Harold B., ed. "Linguistic Geography," in *Readings in Applied English Linguistics*. Second edition. New York: Appleton-Century-Crofts, 1964.

Anderson, Wallace L., and Norman G. Stageberg, eds. "Linguistic Geography," in *Introductory Readings on Language*. New York: Holt, Rinehart and Winston, Inc., 1962.

Atwood, Elmer Bagby. *A Survey of Verb Forms in the Eastern United States*. Ann Arbor, Michigan: University of Michigan Press, 1953.

————. *The Regional Vocabulary of Texas*. Austin: University of Texas Press, 1962.

Bloomfield, Leonard. "Dialect Geography," Chapter 19 of *Language*. New York: Holt, Rinehart and Winston, 1933.

Francis, W. Nelson. "Regional Variety in English," in *The English Language: An Introduction*. New York: W. W. Norton & Company, Inc., 1965.

Gleason, H. A., Jr. "Variation in Speech," in *An Introduction to Descriptive Linguistics*. Revised edition. New York: Holt, Rinehart, and Winston, Inc., 1961.

————. "Language Variation," in *Linguistics and English Grammar*. Garden City, N. Y.: Doubleday and Company, Inc., 1960.

Joos, Martin. "The Five Clocks," *International Journal of American Linguistics*, April 1962.

Kurath, Hans. *A Word Geography of the Eastern United States*. Ann Arbor: University of Michigan Press, 1949.

Kurath, Hans, and Raven I. McDavid, Jr., *The Pronunciation of English in the Atlantic States*. Ann Arbor: University of Michigan Press, 1961.

Lehmann, Winfred P. *Historical Linguistics: An Introduction* (Chapter 8). New York: Holt, Rinehart and Winston, Inc., 1962.

Marckwardt, Albert H. *American English*. New York: Oxford Press, 1959.

McDavid, Raven I., Jr., in *Modern Composition,* Book Six, ed. Edwin Sauer. New York: Holt, Rinehart and Winston, Inc., 1966.

————. "The Dialects of American English," in W. Nelson Francis, *The Structure of American English*. New York: Ronald Press, 1958.

Mencken, H. L. *The American Language,* abridged by Raven I. McDavid, Jr., with the assistance of David Maurer (especially Chapter VII). New York: Alfred A. Knopf, 1963.

Pyles, Thomas. *Words and Ways of American English*. New York: Random House, 1952.

Reed, Carroll. *American Dialects*. Cleveland and New York: World Publishing Company, 1967.

INDEX

67

ISBN 0-8141-1206-4

Discovering American Dialects